Traveling Through My Mind:

VOLUME 1

ELMO KELLEY

Traveling Through My Mind: Volume 1

iUniverse books may be ordered through booksellers or by contacting:

iUniverse
1663 Liberty Drive
Bloomington, IN 47403
www.iuniverse.com
844-349-9409

Because of the dynamic nature of the Internet, any web addresses or links contained in this book may have changed since publication and may no longer be valid. The views expressed in this work are solely those of the author and do not necessarily reflect the views of the publisher, and the publisher hereby disclaims any responsibility for them.

Any people depicted in stock imagery provided by Getty Images are models, and such images are being used for illustrative purposes only.
Certain stock imagery © Getty Images.

ISBN: 978-1-6632-3048-5 (sc)
ISBN: 978-1-6632-3049-2 (e)

Library of Congress Control Number: 2022900517

Print information available on the last page.

iUniverse rev. date: 01/07/2022

CONTENTS

CREDITS

---•◆•---

There are many people I would love to thank for making this book possible.

First I need to thank my wife Barbara for putting up with me for the past 20 years and encouraging me to write more and sharing some of my poems with her colleagues over at A.B. Miller High school . You have always been a rock of support in my crazy life.

I would love to thank my two kids, Kendall and Carson for being an inspiration not only for my poems but for giving me a part of my childhood and energy that I know I need to have in my own life.

I would love to thank my sister in law Jan, for pushing me to finally getting all of the hundreds of poems I have written and getting them made into a book. She has worked hard to make sure that I get this done before any more time passes. She must really like my poems for her to want to get them published! I dedicate this book to you, Rest i8n peace dear sister .

I would love to thank my good friend Norma, who believed in my poetry when I didn't think they were really that good, and inspired me to keep writing .You have motivated me to keep going even when I thought there was nothing left for me to write about.

Micheal Jimenez - thank you for the amazing artwork in this book, including the outstanding front cover Your friendship is also a work of art !

Daphne Rodriguez - thank you for the amazing drawing of the heart and bandaid . You are the most amazing teenager I know !

I would like to thank all of my friends who have taken time from their busy days to read my poems and share how it has made them feel. Your encouragement has been like wind that has pushed me to continue to write.

Last and definitely not least I would love to thank my parents. Although my mom sadly passed away two years ago, she was able to encourage me a not only a teacher but as a writer, one of the sweetest moments of my life was being able to write a poem for her that she loved, which later I would read at her funeral.

I thank my dad for being the creative mastermind who would help me in my college days with my term papers and using an amazing writing style, that got me started down my path of being a poet.

FORWARD

I always look forward to reading Elmo's poems; he keenly observes and processes situations (positive and negative) and then frames them in ways that are entertaining, relatable, and thought-provoking. Elmo's scope and use of creativity encourages and urges one to consider ideas, experiences, and circumstances from diverse perspectives; he dares you to explore! His writing has provided moments of comfort, humor, and inspiration and I am thrilled that he is (finally 😊) sharing his gift and talent with the world.

Carrie Rodgers, friend and colleague at work

FIRST STOP:
The Pandemic

Never in our life time has one event completely changed our world and how we live . During this pandemic, we have had to reinvent our style of living, how we interact with others and find new ways of doing things . It was also a time I wrote more poems than I had ever done before. Maybe spending more time at home helped with that. These poems written during this time, are my response to the pandemic and how our world will forever be changed . No mask needed as you travel through these poems.

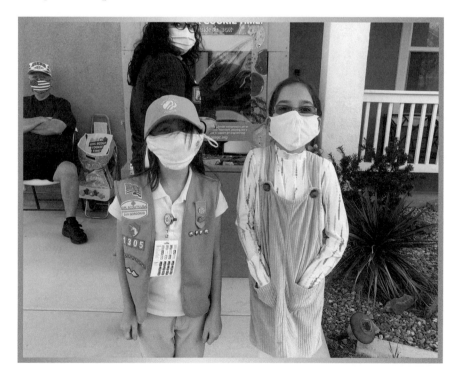

My daughter Kendall and her best friend Emily selling girl scout cookies.

Uncertainty

My thoughts are like puffs of smoke
scattered in many directions
Drifting off and changing form
Some darken others fade from view
Question marks decorate my horizon
And the only thing I know for certain
Is that I don't know what to expect
I can see myself smiling through the flowers
And then cry as locust eat them away
This life has few guarantees
Other than we will all end up
Lying down in the same ground
Enjoy the moments that bring you joy
Try to carry them in your heart
Because nothing lasts forever
Abandon reading a script for your life
Improvise, live each moment as brand new
But believe that love can be a map
That turns chaos into happiness
And question marks into periods
Enjoy the uncertainty
Because not knowing where you're going
Is more than half of the fun

And So It Ends

I could see the paint slowly peeling
The lights flickering on and off
furniture being removed
Fixtures plucked off the walls
Weeks before the building finally closed

I saw the writing on the wall
Which had lately been merely words
Faintly adorning the ceiling
Signaling that it was time to put
This dream back into storage

No last goodbyes as
The curtain falls upon the stage
And sadly, so it ends
What can I look forward to
What changes will I have to make

The new normal
Doesn't feel normal to me
I begin looking for what I can build
After much has been destroyed

Why did this happen ?
Will I ever get an answer
Silence fills my echos again
And so it ends again.

Quarantine

One more padlock on my door
One more message to ignore
Self imposed with no end in sight
Every day feels just like night
Six feet apart they say is the rule
Life has turned impossibly cruel
I'm on an island all to myself
The solitary book on a dusty old shelf
I refuse to share my prolonged agony
Scared of what people will actually see
There might be a day I will talk to you
Just don't ask me when, I have no clue
As hard as I try to wash away this hurt
There always remains some lingering dirt
I place a mask to cover the pain
In quarantine Is where I will remain
When I can learn to smile I will be back
To see all colors not just white and black

Connectivity Issues

The messages to her aren't loud or clear
The words she's saying I can barely hear
Always attempting to reconnect
feels like our love is circumspect
Time and again I message her name
always ends up being the same
Today you can talk to people on the moon
While being locked up in your empty room
But lately she feels a million miles away
More distantly lonely with each passing day
Distracted by things going on nearby
I see her in the room, camera on standby
Her absence recorded but always denied
says she is here but has obviously lied
All the technology in the world won't fix our mess
Going more south that Antarctica I must confess
So I type a last text from my side of the bed
I pray that she answers before she has fled
I see she has turned off her phone one more time
Connectivity issues at the scene of the crime

Soup of Lies

It all started with a warm broth
Steam rising over the top
Enchanting my nostrils
Begging me to take a long taste
Noodles embracing chicken
Carrots mingling with celery
Calling me to come closer
But before I could indulge
More was added
Things I were told would enhance
The aroma and texture
I was hesitant to take a spoonful
But was told it would taste even better
Trust what is in the soup he said
The more that was added the less I believed
Before I knew it,the soup
Looked like a cesspool of chaos
A science experiment gone bad
Just close your eyes and believe
The smell had become toxic
My eyes started to tear up
And I heard him say
Don't believe what you see
This soup is perfect and nothing will be better
I look around me to see
If anyone else was enjoying their soup
Some took spoonfuls
Holding their noses
Like a kid taking bad medicine
Others kept downing it
Like it was 99 cent gasoline
For their expensive car
I was the only one
Who dumped it in the sink
Not believing anything I had heard
And decided to eat a sandwich instead

Broken Windows

Another store set on fire
Followed by a mob of people
Running out with new Vans
Not paid for, empty boxes thrown to the curb
Enjoying an illegal shopping spree
Not knowing what they are doing
Is making this trip through apocalypse
Much uglier and worse
Then the mess they left behind
Donning masks they never wore
During the first epidemic
We are still suffering through
They destroy all they see
Along with other people's dreams
Sadly, those who are protesting
Now are labeled as the bandits
The criminals get away with their loot
Taking advantage of a situation
Making money off of a despair
More common than we ever dreamed
Is this the world we created
And somehow devastated?
Are we all part of this crazy
Everyman for themselves mentality
I see the smoke and tear gas fly
And my own tears fall from my eyes
Our world has shattered like a broken window
If there's any hope we can clean up
Before it's too late for us all?
I would love to see humanity rise up
Use this as a wakeup call
That we are better than this
Finally learn from our repeated mistakes
That we keep making.

SECOND STOP:
Life at School circa 2020

Being a teacher has always been difficult to say the least. But imagine having to teach online to a bunch of second graders from home, with you own kids at home as well. That was quite a challenge! Every day was a new adventure, especially with technology issues, kids getting bored with the new format and rules changing from day to day. By the end of the school year both teachers, students, and parents had experienced enough of distance learning to last a lifetime . But like I always say challenges always make for good poems, and these five about the past school year are some of my favorites I've written recently.

Some of the symbols of teaching during distance learning,
where teachers suddenly became magicians.

The Sad but True Distant Learning Blues

Waking up, I decide to keep my pajamas on
No need to change I won't be teaching too long
Turn on computer logging into Teams again
four kids I can't see are waiting,time to begin
Baby again is screaming in the background
Looking to see if it's mine making that sound
Four weeks in and they are dropping like flies
And here I am constantly wondering why
Time for me to wake up and get a clue
I've got these sad but true distant learning blues
Fighting my kids to do their online work
Feeling each day like more of a jerk
Flood of assignments due every day
But all my kids want to do is to play
Kids are using my cell phone what can I say
When are the laptops heading our way ?
So I sit here pulling all of my hair out
Wondering what Moby Max is all about
Hoping the day will soon return
back to the classroom is where I best learn
But for now we don't get to choose
Suffering through the distant learning blues
I have no idea what next year will bring
10 kids in a classroom should make me sing
Glass partitions abound, no kids can play
Good god almighty there must be another way
But for now I stop dreaming and look ahead
Work smarter not harder is what is being said
So I find another reason for me to booze
Drinking through my distant learning blues

The Magician

Kids come gather round those shiny new screens
To see the amazing magician of your dreams
performing all kinds of jaw dropping tricks
Mesmerizing you all with a flick of my wrists
On this debut performance of the new season
All were excited, with very good reason
I had been gone on a nice summer break
Enjoying vacation with my rabbit named Jake
But now I was ready and eager to share
All I had learned with passion and flair
My first trick for you will astound and amaze
I'm taking attendance with a fiery blaze
Learning new names can cause a big fright
Pronouncing them all and getting some right
Next I will share what we are learning this year
When I looked at my audience, I started to fear
Some were yawning others making weird poses
And I caught a few even picking their noses
Asking my audience to share something cute
Reminding the rest to put themselves on mute
I heard about Roblox, Nintendo,and cats

About mean little sisters and other fun facts
Then my own kids ran screaming onto the stage
Leaving me fuming my face in a rage
But on with the show, I can't stop now
I have many more tricks,so on I must plow
As I looked in the crowd for an assistant or two
To help me with another trick I needed to do
Some kids were walking away from their post
I was losing my audience, my career was toast
Luckily my assistants got them back on task
I needed to finish, I looked for a flask
I learned a few things during this opening show
We definitely do have a long way to go
So I ended my performance to the kids I adore
"I will see you tomorrow we will get to learn more"
As I clicked off the stage I was left wondering how
Will I be able to do this ? Cause I'm not feeling it now
But I know there are thousands of magicians out there
Trying their darnedest because they really do care
So when you walk out on stage on this new scary quest
Do it for all for those kids who deserve your very best

And Now for my Next Trick… : The Magician Part 2

When I slowly turned on my stage for another exhausting day
Was wondering to myself there has to be a better way
The tricks I was using were losing their zeal
The kids and their faces devoid of appeal
9 months of performances were taking their toll
A part of me missing, I was losing my soul
Then a voice in the crowd came in loud and real clear
Yelling,"Why don't you try something new, but do not fear"
I looked to see who was making this stern request
Was our slick sounding boss in an expensive looking vest
Sadly someone who's alien to the classroom for many years
And when I heard what he wanted, it left me with big tears
"Why don't you try and teach three groups at a time,
One with you in the classroom and the other two online?"
I laughed when I heard this silly outlandish dare
Was he serious with this idea that he had to share?
How many hours would my kids be in class?
Was the urgent question that I couldn't let pass
They would be in for 6 hours all wearing a mask
No sharing, no moving all sitting quite still
Like a slow moving Disney ride, very low thrill
Plexiglass partitions on each desk will look quite stellar
The kids will all look like mini Bank of America tellers
My mind was quickly fuming,I was starting to shake
I'm not sure how much more of this nonsense I could take
We have endured bad connections, faulty meetings on Teams
Smoke detectors chirping, and a million babies' screams

And now they want to add more hoops for us to jump
We just want to survive through this one final hump
Why now, what's the hurry?, we have less than eight weeks
But when I looked into his eyes I learned that money always speaks
So a bunch of magicians are all waiting for the final word
Millions of spread rumors is all that we have heard
Can't imagine how many more tricks I will have to perform
But Im learning that this boss rarely likes to inform
Now I look at the amazing kids who could all use a lengthy rest
And I know whatever landmines encountered we will do our very best
So magicians out there stay strong and no moping
Be as strong as those kids who have done a lot of coping
Just like a puff of smoke this will quickly all disappear
And remember summer vacation will surely soon be here

What could possibly go wrong?

Classroom now is 100 percent clean
Desks in perfect rows feels like a dream
Plexiglass barriers covering each one
Individual booths where kids will have fun
No boxes stacked too high to fall on a kid
Floors are sparkling all the dirt Has been rid
Students haven't been here in way too long
I'm ready to start what could possibly go wrong ?
Masked kids start walking in through the door
Here comes one, waiting for seven more
As they each find their seat I remember it's time
To turn on my computer for the ones online
Microsoft teams never seems to go away
Let's hope it works at school I silently pray
Seven more weeks of this, that isn't too long
I let students in what could possibly go wrong ?
Before I know it, it's time for our lunch
But it's a little past 10 they won't eat too much
Students struggle to keep on their masks
Hard to understand what each of them asks
Little movement,no talking their friends far away
I'm sad for them all, don't know what to say
The day almost over it's time to finally abort
Do this all again tomorrow with a different cohort
But I'm proud of the kids for being so strong
No more worrying about what could possibly go wrong?

To Test or not to Teach

To test or not to teach,that is the question
Whether it's better to fill in the bubbles
Of a million mindless questions
Or to actually learn something redeeming
That is our dilemma
Do we instill in our charges with a love of learning?
Or erode them with a feeling that a score is
All that we adore and can embrace?
Our choice, or do we even have one?
Has fallen into a hole like the textbooks
Of a thousand adoptions
Into a sea of lost souls
The pangs of reaching proficient scores
That ultimately decides our fate
Lie in the hands of kids
Who fly through exams
With no regard to what is correct
And decide to make cute patterns
With the bubbles they half fill in
And this we have reached our crux
What are we to do?
Do we try to teach our students on the two weeks
In the year that are devoid of exams
Or do we fix their tests
Before turning them in?

THIRD STOP:
Humor Me

To me humor has always been a kind of medicine I have used to make myself and others feel better. I often use jokes as a way to deal with stress and yes to make others laugh!. Just like writing a poem is an art form, telling a good joke or being funny is an art form as well. If we can't laugh at ourselves, then we are truly missing something in our own life. So please enjoy these trips to the funnier side of my poetry writing.

Seems a lot of my humor and silliness have rubbed off on my son Carson.

All You Need is Love and Hair Clippers

You don't need to be a Paperback Writer
To understand this story of extreme Help
That was needed by a Boy
Whose Day in the Life
Was a long and winding road
It was time for a hair revolution
He didn't want to travel across the universe
Or go here and there and everywhere
To fix his Helter Skelter hair
It was time to Come Together
With his mom the Lovely Rita
To Carry that Weight off his head
I Want to Hold your Hand, mom
Cause this Ticket to Ride
May leave me a Nowhere Man
Oh Darling, she whispered to me
Do You Want to Know a Secret?
When I am done, you will Dig It
Ok, Mom, Don't Let Me Down
With that the Two of Us prayed
And I tried not to Twist and Shout
Clippers buzzing! Just Act Naturally
I hope it's Getting Better
And prayed she wasn't Fixing a Hole
Soon the Lady Madonna was done
Was I going to look like Rocky Raccoon
Or a Fool on the hill?
If you don't like it, we can work it out,
With a Little Help From my Friends
Look in the mirror Tell Me What You See
I Saw Her Standing There
Beethoven wouldn't roll over
It wasn't perfect but I will Let It Be
We Can Work It Out
It Won't Be Long till the barbershop opens
But I Want to Tell you
I Should Have Known Better.
The End

Peninsula of Desire

My old life was getting into terrible ruts
Needed a new beginning but had no guts
I was tired of being like everyone I saw
Wanted to leave the whole world in awe
Saw an interesting description inside of a flier
Make dreams come true on the Peninsula of Desire
Filled out the application, described my request
To be truly amazing and reach level best
A few days later I jumped onto a plane
Headed for a land of beauty, was I insane?
On final approach I heard a bell ringing
Followed by a French voice happily singing
The aircraft landed on a water so blue
Walked off and thanked the amazing crew
Accepted a drink from some cute island chick
Drank it really fast, that should do the trick
Was greeted by a host all dressed in white
With a little companion three feet in height
I heard them talking wondering what they were saying
But couldn't hear a thing from the cool music playing
Also, on the landing which came as a surprise
Was an ancient celebrity in an interesting disguise
Could have sworn it was a lady I had to take note
It must be Julie from that show the Love Boat
With a toast from our host the fun would begin
For once in my life I was ready to win
Back in my bungalow I got a knock on the door
Quickly I answered to see what it was for
It was our host with an accent so cool and thick

He handed me a pill saying this will do the trick
Reminding me sternly don't take more than one
Because if you do, that will end all your fun
Once after taking it, my body started swaying
I have to admit our host wasn't playing
Speedily, I could feel my brain starting to grow
The thoughts in my head were ready to flow
Before I knew it, I was writing a whole book
I was making new dishes; did I learn to cook?
Going outside I glimpse a familiar girl
Who didn't give me a chance in my other world
I walked up to her and tell her two jokes
She raises a smile and some laughter invokes
Without even thinking I turn up the charm
From dork to instant adorable now I am alarmed
We go to a luau to eat and to dance
Where I finally learn all about true romance
At the same time, I'm writing a song in my head
About a guy who spends all day in his bed
Crowds swarmed around me, the talk of the town
Everyone smiling, but I did see one frown
The girl by my side who I'm trying to impress
Had the most beautiful eyes and a sexy red dress
But this pill I have taken had made me ignore
That same lady beside me, the one I adore
I'm talking, I'm joking,I'm having a blast
But with all good things this sadly wouldn't last
The more I was creating the farther she went
Gone after a while like the time that we spent
I had gained popularity I was in fashion

But gone was the lady who gave me much passion
As the pill wore off, I learned my mistake
When you aren't yourself you become a real fake
I walked to the car that was missing the doors
Learning a great lesson, I could have done more
While shaking the hands of my amazing hosts
I thanked them for everything, including their toasts
Before entering the plane, I heard a familiar voice
As I turned around, I had to make a choice
The girl from the luau, time to make amends
If anything at all, wanted to part as good friends
I told her I was sorry, wasn't feeling myself
Was acting real crazy not in good health
She touched my shoulder and said these words
"Although you were cute you acted like a turd."
I had liked you before the night we went out
But I couldn't tell you what this all was about
I would love to see you again I'd enjoy the thrill
But promise to be yourself and don't be a pill!
And with that I held her, and we boarded the plane
I will work on being happy and not be insane
On our way back home, I found it quite funny
I'm a richer from this though I have much less money

Throw Ex Hubby Off the Plane

Let me try real hard to explain
Why I threw ex hubby off of the plane
I should have left him there at the altar
But way back then my brain had faltered
Then dem darn kids came along
And things quickly went from bad to wrong
Our love quickly started to fade
From being his wife to full time maid
Socks and underwear on the floor
Legos, Lincoln logs, and so much more
Over the years we started to lose touch
playing more video games not talking as much
Turned out he had found a brand new fan
Someone in a pink bow named Ms. Pac Man
It came to a point we decided to call it quits
So like an exotic dancer we did the splits
After all that it, was worse than old baloney
Falling to give me all of my alimony
We instead decided to go on an exotic trip
So I did my best to bite my fat lip
Flying to Hawaii should be a lot of fun
But somewhere over the Pacific, I was done
When the stewardess asked if he wanted nuts
I told her he never had those, that took guts
He got so irate I could see the steam rise
Leaving his seat full of hate and despise
Then I witnessed something not seen before
It appeared he was heading straight for the door
My mind started to think and was wondering why
This man was going to jump out and fly
I ran with all my might to halt his big jump
My eyes couldn't believe my throat in a lump
As I grabbed for his jacket I heard him say
Please let me go, my insurance will pay
So I let go of him and he flew through the air
For a few seconds he yelled in despair
Then the parachute soon came into glorious life
And now I was happy to be his ex wife

22

Drama Queen Incorporated

It's time to worry, it's time to cry
Blow out of proportion for no reason why
Airing my laundry for the world to see
Suffering through another Catastrophe
I'm pulling my hair out one by one
Soon will be balder than a hamburger bun
The reason you ask it's plain to see
My furry little cat won't talk to me
If that's not enough I'll tell you more
No one will message me I'm being ignored
Oh no the tears are coming quick
Mascara running, I'm gonna be sick !
Yes my world feels like it's ending
I'm not making this up,nor am I pretending
I'll post it on Facebook, send it to Twitter
I guess I've slowly become very bitter
I've been told to calm down not be so extreme
But it happens so much if you now what I mean
I apologize profusely for sharing my views
Just wait for my story on the 11 o'clock news

That One Patch Of Grass

There is little he can do to save that patch
Where once was grass but now is ash
The jungle has turned into a craterless moon
Which women would feel and quickly swoon
But he continues to try and save that lump
With comb and oil he waters that stump
He hopes one day some turf will sprout
Multiply into a fair amount
But Charlie Brown this won't occur
Your days of growth are gone for sure
This monument he thought, could be saved
With comb-overs it might be paved
But I am afraid for that one patch of grass
Its finest days have long since passed
Kojak, Warbucks, and Picard all survived
On heads were no hair did reside
So by removing those strands is not a sin
Because sometimes by losing you actually win

Forces of Nature Ruined

As I was sitting watching this movie
Which was rather comic and never gloomy
I get a text from an old friend
Who made it seem his life would end?
I push the pause as Ben is speaking
About blurbs in novels that he is seeking
My friend tells me of woes I can't explain
Worse than a bird being sucked in a plane
I felt compelled to hear his sad story
My friend was despondent, and this sounded gory
A few tears fell as I listened to this dork
More upsetting than missing prongs on a fork
He had dealt with a day full of bad drama
Maybe he needed the help of the Dali Lama
I wish I could reach out and give him a hug
Cause sadly he thought that all he does is bug
The storms the turmoil's we all have to endure
All happened to him in one quick blur
Although he ruined my movie, I must admit
I was glad I could listen and not once did quit
From being the friend, he really does need
Now back to the movie I did my good deed
These forces of nature sometimes bring us closer
But now I am glad that this is all over.

The Deep Sleep

The alarm clock screams, it's time to wake up
But she continues to snore like a newborn pup
The ground starts to shake the tv is blaring
But eyes do not open, her bed she's not sharing
Sleeps through a steam train chugging along
Deep in a long trance and snoring her song
Could doze through a poem I'm writing about sleep
And all I can do is count millions of sheep
I'm afraid even Metallica couldn't wake her now
Could I find some explosives, make them go pow?
Was thinking of buying her a huge boom box clock
One that could give her an electrical shock
Certainly, she would stay dead to the world
In that comatose state this poor little girl
From the other room I hear the sawing of logs
Much more louder than a battalion of frogs
I will wait for my lumberjack to finally awake
According to the seismograph it's a 9.1 quake
So, if you see a house nearby that loses its roof
It' probably mine with the snoring, sleeping goof.

FOURTH STOP:
The Holidays

The holidays are truly a special time where we get to spend time with our family and friends. Many times we learn more interesting about ourselves and others . I often wonder about the true meanings of each holiday and often will write a poem to go with the celebration. Now let's see what the holidays can also bring.

Holiday memories with my family, a great time to celebrate and also dress up as a turkey.

Lonely Girl On Valentine's

She listens to the one message from her mom on the empty machine
Telling her that not having a guy isn't the end of the world
She turns on the tv and settles in for a fun filled episode of Extreme Doghouse Makeover Home Edition
Plops a Hungry man into her well used microwave
The phone ringing breaks the vacuumed silence
She frantically picks up
Hearing a deep sultry sexy male voice on the other end tell her that Direct Tv has an awesome movie package that ends tomorrow and she needs to act now
The phone drops from her sweat dripped hands
Tears begin to flow down her frustrated saddened face
She dreads this day every year
No reason to celebrate Valentines
When the only man in your life
Is the Pillsbury Doughboy
She attempts to dry the tears
That have made a pool next to the space
Where the Mashed Potatoes go
Her Life has been consumed with finding a man
But maybe she has something she needs to find first
When she looks in the mirror at her beat red face
She determines she needs to find something else first
She knows what it is as she looks into her drying eyes

Turkey for Thanksgiving

He sits at the dinner table and contemplates
Who is more of a Turkey this Thanksgiving
The brown juicy bird with a brilliant deep tan
Relaxing on top of the dinner table
Or the guy with a knife and fork in hand
Waiting to carve and destroy his savory meal
Was only yesterday he was complaining again
About wearing a mask when buying this bird
On a unusually windy fall day
And getting into a tug of war
Over the remaining toilet paper roll
at the local Costco with a lady twice his age
And half his height
Then waiting in the endless.
Siberian like checkout line
For what seemed like days
Disdain on his face as he navigated his way through the parking lot
Like a soldier through a minefield
Something hit him .. not a car, not debris
A force much stronger while at a red light
Here he is upset, the day before thanksgiving
While he has a job, his health, and family
Who care about him a great deal
Now he looks at his meal and realizes
Yes the world has thrown some potholes
Into a crazy obstacle course
Complete with spike strips,
Hoops set ablaze
Randomly falling platforms
With snake infested pits
That would even make Indiana Jones cry
But he has survived them all
He is not the turkey on thanksgiving
There is plenty to be grateful for
He sits at the dinner table
Surrounded by his immediate family
They hold hands
And pray for all that they do have
Thankful to all be together and safe
Then the power goes out
And I finally realize
Who the true turkey is on thanksgiving

Christmas is Over

All the presents have been unwrapped
All the hinny paper thrown away
I look around and I begin to wonder
Has anything really changed ?
Does everyone go back to being
The way they were before
Only thinking about themselves
And acting all absurd
Now that Christmas is over
I hope that peace and love remain
Not thrown out with the tissue paper
Or sent out with the train
Let's stretch out this season
And give gifts every day of the year
Those that you can't buy in a store
Or order on Amazon
But come from deep inside

New Year's Resolutions

Better than a Life in prostitution
More lively than drafting the constitution
It is time to come to some conclusions
And write some New Year's resolutions
Let's begin with the time I waste online
From Playing dominoes to losing my mind
An hour turns into an entire freakin day
So Goodbye computer, lets flush it down the drain
I want to work on why I'm so shy
I get scared of someone with no real reason why
I'm going to say hi to the next person I meet
Except for the guy with no shirt across the street
This year I will learn to play guitar
Decide to learn, "When you Wish Upon a Star"
If I'm lucky I will join a rock band
That even Simon Cowell could kinda stand
I wasn't to finish this poem soon
This paper has run out of room
So my resolutions are done I can't deny
Let's finish them all before July

Winter Snows

Her love truly reminds me
Of the harsh but beautiful winter snows
Furiously cold and brutal
But gracefully falling all over me
Leaving a pure blanket
Thick as my heart which yearns for her
The more I look at what surrounds me
The more I want to stay forever
But also fearful
that when the snows melt
what lies underneath
may show me a different landscape
One that as spring emerges
Will transform who she is
But despite her constant flurries
I embrace those snowflakes
Create snow angels in her presence
From now until the end of time.

FIFTH STOP:
Destination Heartache

Life unfortunately is full of heartaches. It can be a result of losing a loved one, ending a relationship, getting fired from a job or a million other reasons. For me heartaches are easy to write about and also very relatable to others. Writing poetry has afforded me with a cost effective way of dealing with my turmoils without needing a therapist. Have some Kleenex handy as we travel through some heartache.

Sadly a bandaid can never heal our heartaches, but for me writing has helped a great deal.

Fool's Mirage

Traveling down an apocalyptic deserted highway there she stood
Much like a gasoline station in the desert
She quickly comes back into full view
She had disappeared not long ago
So I pull over and let her in
Once again entranced by her smile
Wanting to know where she had been
Each question I ask seems to rekindle
A fire that spread like warm peanut butter
On a piece of burnt toast
Her mystery once again in full bloom
But those flowers sprout
more voids than answers
The more she speaks I feel
Her words starting to chip away
At my heart like a frenzied woodpecker
Soon I feel guilty for crimes I haven't committed
And bombarded with attacks
Like a pirate ship with more holes
Than a miniature golf course
The more I drive the more I realize
This is not going to work out
She makes more demands
Than a Cuban hijacking a plane
When I respond back I don't hear a thing
I rub my eyes and look her way
But there is no one there
My stomach had been a bouquet of knots
slowly working on untying themselves
Sadly some things aren't what they appear
You paint a pretty picture
You look for the best in every situation
But often what you get back
Is a fools mirage
A sad reality that disappears from view
But lingers in your heart forever
I drive on looking for solace
But sad at the things left behind

You Can't Count on Me

She tightly grips the side of the canyon
Screaming for dear mercy
As her fingernails
Quickly lose their handle on the side
And all I can do is finish eating my popcorn
Laughing as she falls below to her death
Screaming her head off
Much like Hans Gruber in Diehard
I quickly flip to another movie
Hoping to find something else to eliminate
My thoughts of all of those needing my help
My sage advice,that usually goes ignored
Wasted upon friends who find themselves
On busses that can't slow down,
Airplanes with a bomb strapped underneath
Or a huge boat sinking in the frigid Atlantic
I enjoy each scene from my sofa
Relishing the fact that I won't help them anymore
It's each person for themselves
Each cry for help met with indifference
When were they there for me ?
Did they ever comfort me
When my home planet was destroyed
By the powerful lasers on the Death Star
Visit me when a huge shark
Almost ate me up?
Or give me a hug
When my parents left me home alone
So please don't count on me
No matter what you do
I will hopefully see you
In a movie real soon

Silence

An endless vacuum of desolation
Envelope the last words spoken.
The reply never given, hangs over me
Like a hot air ballon stuck on a cloud
The sound pierces through my ears
Constantly banging like a hammer
Louder which each swing
A perpetual unrelenting pounding
Echoing, reverberating
But as cold as dry ice to my skin
Nothing hurts more to me
Than the words that are never spoken
The unfillable void that separates
Two people, which time seems to expand
Where once a bridge stood
Firm, strong and connected
Now A canyon carved with winds
Of silence continues to flourish
I yell in hopes of an answer
And all I get is my own voice
Screaming back at me

Laundromat

I want to wash you out of my life
So I take my clothes for a spin
Ending up at an all night laundromat
Where I can remove the messes I have made
Throwing in my first load
I add ample amounts of detergent into the washer
Watching the wet clothes spin
Like a hamster on his first dosage of crack
Adding quarters to the machine
I slowly realize some stains
Will be permanent witnesses to my mistakes
And point me out in a police line up
Only god can provide stain remover
For the guilt I can't erase
I feel the tears tumbling down
As the clothes make it through the spin cycle
Some garments come out as good
As the day i bought them
Others I decide to keep
As they are like old teddy bears
Comforting me, without judgement
Hours later I came out of washing machine heaven
Realizing I still have much to clean
And needing many more quarters
To feed into the machine
And continue cleaning my life away

Someone Almost Cared

She was just about to give a dollar
To the man with a tattered sign on the freeway
She decided against it
Thought that man was looking for drinking money
Sped off and never looked back
If only his sign had been decorated better

He saw her crying a river of tears at the office
Found a Kleenex in his pocket
Kept it where it was as she continued to cry
Not his fault she is upset
Maybe the office needs a second water cooler
California in a drought we need the rain

An old lady had problems getting her car to start
Her 74 Ford Maverick lay comatose
He had jumper cables in the trunk
And decided to leave them there
Along with the lady cranking away
Somethings he thought, should never
be brought back to life

The Cheesiest Love Lost Poem Ever

Walking along the shore I once again cry
I'm probably the worlds most pitiful guy
The love of my life has suddenly faded from view
Leaving me sadder than a missing new shoe
Her eyes could light my house missing it's power
Her touch requires me to take another shower
Now all I hear is her voice echoing to me
As I look into the ocean there is nothing I see
I would have climbed Mount Everest just to see her face
Would have boarded a rocket deep into space
But there isn't a chance there isn't a reason
Like swim trunks in Christmas, it's just out of season
I continue to walk and kick up some sand
Trying my best but I can't understand
I was holding on tight to her beautiful rope
Until she pulled it away and I fell like a dope
Her laughter still ringing deep inside my ears
I think it is time To drink a few beers
Some day I will try to win her back
Write her a poem, will give it a crack
Put down in words what she means to me
Doubtful that this will make her finally see
My Hail Mary pass will go incomplete
My heart has been tackled in defeat
As the cheese on this poem starts to get moldy.
I end it right there and move on quite boldly

SIXTH STOP:
Relationships

Good relationships with other people are very difficult to maintain. When two people who are different in many ways try to get together, it often doesn't work out. People see things differently, have different values, the list is endless. Sometimes you need to accept people for who they are. These poems are about to struggles with relationships you may have with others, and possibly with yourself

A relationship with someone can sometimes feel like a tug of war, except no one really wins. You just get tired when it's all over.

He said / She said

Her eyes penetrate the outer reaches of my soul
His bloodshot eyes keep looking at my boobs
He shared his life story as she clung to every word
She stared at the clock hoping something would
mute this nerd
He enjoyed his meal that was fancy and surprising
she couldn't believe they were eating at Burger King
He walked her to his chariot, all shinning and new
She made it safely to his 82 Subaru
He blasted melodious music from a time long ago
She almost had a coma while listening to Manilow
He dropped her off at her place which didn't look bad
She regretted having him know the location of her pad
He gave her a hug and said, I will call you soon
She prayed he'd forgot and begged to the moon
He drove home smiling, remembering fondly of his date
She went to get a Patron and drown her fate
So why do we learn and what is the theme ?
What's good for one may be another's bad dream

Decriminalize

She slams the door in my face
and as my nose feels the pain of the wood,
I was once again on my own ...
Walking out from her front lawn
I see countless dying flowers
Laying on the ground pleading for water
Knowing their chances were next to zero
Of ever coming back to life
Crossing the street, I almost get run over
By a speeding black mustang
That only goes faster as it leaves a trail
Of smoke surrounding my body
Sadly, I wish the car would have hit me
Since I had already had my heart
Taken out of me a few minutes before
She told me she would only
want to see me ever again
If I was floating under the swimming pool
As I look up at the clouds, I see a formation
That looks like an egg separating into two
The eggs shells are smaller dissipating clouds
And quickly move as far away from each
Other as they possibly can
I Approach my apartment complex
And I find a dog peeing onto a fire hydrant
Enjoying its shower all over a once
Dry and happy monument
As I open my own door, I wonder

Should I report this crime
Of the heart that has wounded me
People have gone to jail for far less
And sadly, getting dumped is not a
criminal act even if done maliciously
I slowly close the door
And wonder if I should open any others
The silence will now be my medicine
And I try to move on.

Rollercoaster

Every single time I jump off this ride
My hair stands up as straight
As a six-day old French fry
And my stomach joins me sometime
Later the following week
My heart in a perpetual butterfly effect
Screams at me for doing this again
This will be the last time I promise myself
A little while later I am back on the ride
Asking myself why am I doing this?
Are the thrills worth the price of knowing
That the jubilation is short lived
And where I end up is the same place, I began
This time it will be different
I know what to expect
Some of the best times in my life
Were in that amazing roller coaster
Life's colors were a little brighter
The blood pumping a little richer
The lessons learned a little more meaningful
Time to go up again
And yes, eventually down.

Don't exaggerate

I look into your ocean deep blue eyes
And tell you I would walk the ends
Of the world to be by your side
And Immediately you laugh at me
Telling me not to exaggerate
I edit my statement saying
I would cross the street for you
Provided there was a crosswalk
Because getting a jaywalking ticket
Is a risk I can't take at my advanced age
Then I tell you that you're more beautiful
Than the moon on a clear star adorned night
Again you look at me funny
So I revise my comment to,
you're better looking than my lawn after I mow it
I would take you to Paris for an
amazing romantic weekend
Quickly changes to I would drive you to
McDonalds for a quarter pounder with cheese
And you're the smartest person I've ever met
Transforms into I think you could give a
Third grade a run for their money on Jeopardy
When you're with someone who
takes your breath away
Sometimes they can handle a
few clouds in the sky
But never the whole mansion floating above
So when your breath is taken away
Just tell them your not too bad to look at instead

Looking At You

I stare deeply into your saddened eyes
And try remembering when happiness played in them
I see time has eroded your smile
Leaving a frown not even a bodybuilder could lift
We used to laugh at every joke
But even the last comic standing
Couldn't resurrect a chuckle
The wrinkles, the grey hairs
Are like battlegrounds all with dying soldiers
There are a million things I need to say to you
But I know you wouldn't hear me out
You have closed yourself to the entire world
The song is still playing
But you left the building before the first chorus
Looking at you is so hard to do
I know you should be fighting back
But you take each punch like Rocky in the 4th movie
So I turn off the light look away from the mirror
And pretend that I never saw you in the first place

SEVENTH STOP:
Love is In The Air

Love is the most difficult emotion to describe, it can make us sing and also make us cry. It is something we all yearn for and sometimes afraid when it actually comes. There are so many forms of love, I could easily have a book of poems on that subject alone. But here are some of my favorites that I have written.

My daughter Kendall with her first "boyfriend" all these years later they are still friends.

Love is....

I stare out through a dirty window
Probably not cleaned since I last smiled
Trying to figure out what love is..
Maybe love is like an ocean, deep, endless
And always waiting for us to enter
But love are also the waves
That come crashing down on us
Even when we are prepared to face them
Love is jumping out of an airplane
Not knowing where we are going to land
Love is the parachute that doesn't open
Till it's way too late
Love is winning a million dollars in the lottery
When only playing one ticket
Love are the taxes you pay afterwards
That leave you just as penniless as before
Love is safely navigating through rush hour traffic
On the way to the airport
Love is realizing you left your luggage at the hotel
Suddenly, The window finally is cleaned
And I can clearly see you
Love is knowing you will always be here
Love is fearing you will forget who I am

Kisses Anyone?

As soon as my eyes met hers
I knew I had met my match
My heart was caught in her net
And as I came closer
I knew I would love to serve her
A million passionate kisses
And before I knew it
I was hitting her with a volley
Of them one after another
You could hear the smacking
As we both made contact
In our own little court
Sweat began to cover our faces
As we kept going
And not trying to make a racket
The intensity was overwhelming
And we lost our breaths
This was not a game
But love in its truest form
When it was all finished
We both drank a whole bottle of water
We shook our tired hands
Gathered our tennis rackets
And we decided to finally kiss
Each other for the first time

Butterflies

Sometimes as I am talking to you they come
Quickly invading my stomach
Like aliens trying to find a new planet
To finally call their home
After light years of travel across galaxies
They reach their destination
But they don't attack
They do stunt shows across my heart
Moving and dancing like acrobats
Each move more death defying than the last
I feel their every jump, breathe life into me
Increasing, my heartbeat racing faster
But never finding a way to escape
Enjoying their routines of love
With dances to places new and exciting
Butterflies flying and swarming my soul
Leaving me helpless but wanting them more

One Sick Kiss

One sick kiss from you is worth the pain
I write it all and try to explain
Getting pneumonia would be worth Our lips meeting
While battling this cold that's giving me a beating
I am dizzy, I'm a blur
You're the medicine that will help me endure
It's sad but also perfectly true
It's worth the price to get this flu
And as I lay here sick in bed,
that kiss from you I will not dread
I would battle a million colds,
take Ibuprofen till I get old
So, if I ever get a nasty flu
your love is what will pull me through
And in your Kleenex covered bed,
our under the weather love will be fed
I sneeze again this is the end.

Of Rainbows and Unicorns

Life, that constant never-ending journey
Much like a game of Pac-Man
Being repeatedly chased
Through an endless maze
And hoping to make it to another day
Someone pauses this game
Allowing me to eat a few ghosts
Eliminate a couple of torments
And let me enjoy a new landscape
Surrounded by rainbows and unicorns
Where orange trees blossom
Providing me infinite glasses of juice
Let me frolic in the playground of happiness
Welcome the music of a thousand 80's bands
Which become the soundtrack to my life
I want to lose track of the number of times
You've said you love me
As those words have covered my heart
With shiny new grass,
Fragrant flowers, and a river of new hope
I can now clearly see better
What life has thrown at me
And can't wait for what's yet to come.

Testimony

I stand before you now
Proudly proclaiming how I feel
I look into your ocean eyes
And prove my case is real
First upon the stand
Is my one and only heart
Each day it holds more love for you
A million more than from the start
Next we hear from my enormous mind
That is constantly thinking of you
Amazed at how deep your thoughts go
Please never leave me far behind.
Finally my soul pleads a solid case
Knowing there's no one who can replace
Your spirit and your being
All written on that beautiful face
All parts of me have spoken
I now await my sentence
You have given my life new meaning
New breath runs through my lungs
I am guilty of truly loving you
Your love is where I belong

EIGHTH STOP:
Hope and Happiness

The world is full of negativity and can be very bleak. It is amazing how one kind word from someone can often be the difference from someone having a terrible day and instead having it be wonderful. These poems are my way of taking a bad situation and trying to make it full of hope.

Sometimes smiling and hanging out with an old friend brings me a lot of hope and happiness.

The Little Things

We sulk, we worry, we wonder why
And get upset until we cry
The road ahead is often bleak
So many things we need to tweak
Forgetting that life is full of wonders
Often concentrating on just the blunders
But you have to look behind those clouds
And find the things that make you proud
It's time to enjoy those little things
The ones that make you laugh and sing
The good morning message from a friend
Which quickly helps your heart to mend
The hugs your kids will always give
Pumps you with blood and makes you live
Sadly all we hear is heartbreaking news
People keep fighting with conflicting views
So if you can please stop for a second
Look for the joys that often beckon
The student who tells you, you're the best
The all night Sylvester Stallone movie fest
Those little things will help you smile
And keep us from going crazy for a while

Flower in the Rain

Dark storm clouds fast approaching
Zeroing in once again over my head
I look at them and I realize
There's is nothing in them I dread
As the rain does its best to dampen me
I look at that one flower in the rain
Basking in the darkness outside
Making me see true beauty
Her petals as vibrant as 80s neon
It's resounding strength battles
The torrent that pounds her
But remains standing firm
I have no real fears
Like that flower in the rain
Each day is a struggle, a war
That I will ultimately win
It is only by being tested
That we find out who we are
And I smile as another
Hurricane comes to try
And wash my hopes away.

Blanket of Sadness

One day without a warning
A thick heavy blanket fell over me
Felt like weights from the local gym
Pushing the happiness from me
As hard as I tried to pull it away
It tattooed me like a second skin
Why is it there I ask my self
What is making me feel like crying now?
I am surrounded by happiness
By laugher and love
But that only tightens the grip
This blanket has on me
Then the old mantra is heard
If things were different
My life would be better
The blanket almost starts to choke me
There must be a way to escape
I slowly pull the covers
And for some reason they finally
Fall to the floor
I hear the birds singing
Instead of seeing the one dark cloud
In that sky following me
I feel the rays of the sunlight
The laughter and hope
you always bring me
Life has a way of making us fall
Faster than jumping out of a plane
But enjoy even those moments
When you can't even lift a smile
We all have blankets that are hard
to pull off
That need to stay on the bed
Keep them for as long as needed
And one day they may come off.

How Does a Moment Last Forever?

Windmills in his mind start to slow down
Memories like old photographs
Lose their vibrant colors
Some completely torn off the page
The years have created chasms
That desperately want to push delete
On all of those memories
He attempts to salvage his first love
Researches old smells found
In perfume bottles
At the fragrance counter
Taking in the smells
Looking for the one that she wore
50 years before
He sprays some Guerlain in the air
And instantly remembers her face
The scent invades his nostrils
And takes him back to his first car
With her sitting right next to him
Now if he could remember the song
That was playing on the radio
Countless number of tunes

Blare their melodies through the speakers
And then He hears it
The song they would always sing together
Right before going to bed
Almost a lullaby, soothing
Wishing her sweet angel
A Night full of wonderful sleep
Yes a moment Can last forever
A dream can live on
If we keep it safe in our heart
Locked and secure
With a backup copy
In case the winds of time
Try to erode them
Now I look in my mirror
And fear the day when I forget
Who I am looking at
Writing this all down
Before it is too late
And the relentless tide takes
My biggest most beautiful gift,
Knowing who I am

The Dead End

All of a sudden and without a warning
The beautiful freeway adorned
With roses and jaw dropping scenery
was barricaded with an ugly dead end
A well worn sign shot up with bullet holes
Massive cobwebs and misspelled graffiti
Stared me in the eye like a gunslinger
Ready to take back what was his
I couldn't turn back now
No way I could reverse my course
And come to terms with the new landscape
Joy transformed itself into salty tears
Had I made a wrong turn ?
Failed to see a sign telling me to
Transition onto another freeway ?
I didn't see a vehicle anywhere
Maybe I had sped too fast
The price paid for enjoying a trip
But realizing the journey is over
So I press on the gas with all my might
Obliterating the dead end sign
Knowing that forward is the only option left
Things may never be as beautiful again
As I zoom forward to my next location

Helicopter

Time once again to take a trip
And float over her to see what's going on
Up into the clouds I go
Quietly making my way to her
Putting the blades on silent mode
I watch what is going on
Hoping she makes the right choice
Can see the worry on her face
As I zoom in for a closer look
Hard to believe she's all grown up
That not long ago I decided
What clothes she would wear
What she would have for breakfast
Now she makes all the choices
Many I do not agree with
However, this is her life
I would shoot down anyone that hurts her
But in the end, she would shoot me down
Her happiness and safety are my priority
But it's time for me to fly away
And let her come to me when she needs it
I will be just another foolish observer
Proud of what I have seen her become
Excited of where she is going
I quickly fly out of the horizon
Landing safely back at the heliport again.

Castaway

As she jumped off the plane
She screamed, I need some time
Free falling and landing on a deserted island
Knowing that she craved to be alone
Surrounded by ocean water and palm trees
She embraced her departure from what she loved
Now she needed to find something else
,herself, something as lost as
Sunshine in a traffic jam of clouds
What does she look for first ?
The ocean waves provide her music
Reminding her that everything comes back
Then close to a coconut tree
She sees a volleyball
And resists giving it a name and a face
She is alone and wants to stay that way
Leaving it in it's box
Over time she realizes
That to love means to start with herself
To be able to battle the wars in life
You must first arm yourself
Embrace the palm trees,your surroundings
A smile comes back to her face
There was a purpose to all of this
She knew she was ready to return
to the journey she had left behind
After embarking on a more important one
The plane picked her up
But she had a feeling
She might be back here again

FINAL STOP:
Special People

My life has been blessed with some amazing people who have not only helped me through many struggles but have inspired me in different ways. These people have played a part in defining me and making mw want to get up each day and do my best. I am blessed to have them in my life. These poems are dedicated to you.

Beautiful Princess (Kendall's poem)

From the moment I first held her.
And watched her roll across the room
I knew this girl would change my life
Her eyes full of happiness
Energy flowing through her body
Unmatched, infectious, and radiating
Put a warm blanket over my heart
She will talk to anyone which is great
as strangers instantly become friends
Which also kinda scares me
But I know she will always come back to me
Even if I have to beg a few times
With a cookie or a long pleaasseeee
As she grows I have seen her become
A savvy diplomatic negotiator
Making deals for staying up later
And plea bargains for toys she doesn't need
Her never say die attitude
Has made her overcome many obstacles
And shine like the moon on a clear day
She can ride a bicycle
Sing an amazing song
Help me clean the house
Swim partway across a pool
And make me the proudest dad around
One day princess you will take care of me
But for now I enjoy every second
I spend hearing you read
Seeing you sleep
And telling me you love me
The world is your playground
And you are riding it's slides
Climbing its monkey bars
And will always be here to catch you

Carson : Ballad of a Winning Kid

Electricity and power shine in his eyes
Total understanding covers his face
As The little guy finishes his lesson
On common and proper nouns
once again getting 100 percent
Then he tackles a game with Mario in it
Completing the level and laughing hysterically
As Boswer shrieks away back to his castle
80s music playing in the background
Identifying each groups seconds
After the songs blast from his boombox
Hard to imagine a 5 year old
Listening to Foreigner and Styx
And singing that he's hot blooded
Or domo arigatoing Mr. Roboto
His vocabulary rivals that of a high schooler
Sometimes even that of a savvy sailor
When he misses a pin in Wii Bowling
You would think he was turning into the Hulk
As a furious rage envelops his body
So don't get him angry
You wouldn't like him when he's angry
But like a switch being turned on and off

He suddenly transforms back into a sweet kid
Giving you the warmest hugs
He's like an adorable walking smart blanket
The smile he shows in every picture
shows his amazing and cute spirit
But I do feel sorry for next years teacher
When you can read chapter books
And understand how to set up a game console
It's hard to sit through learning the alphabet
And counting numbers up to 10
But when he graduates from high school
In 2 years, it will all be a distant memory
So he makes the most of his amazing gifts
Tackles the world and never surrenders
You are like Mario always jumping around
Finding new ways of getting through levels
Knowing that you will always finish a journey
And start another one with energy and flair
Makes me proud and even more excited
Of all that you will accomplish
And even the headaches you will cause
From my amazing winning son

Why I Love you on Valentines Day(Bubba's Poem)

Quick, find a reason of why you love your wife
On the Super Bowl of love days
Ok I think I got it,
I enjoy the way she sometimes sings
A she goes down the stairs the morning
Nahh, She won't buy that one
She isn't a sucker for that
We,,, Lets try this one on for size
I really enjoy pulling the blankets over her
And pretending Im the Count going,
one, Ahh ahh ahh, two ahh ahh ahh
And so forth until you are snug in your cocoon
Waiting to become a butterfly
Well I know I wouldn't have spent 15 minutes
Fixing the seatbelt on the car, if I didn't love her
And nearly losing a finger in the process
But it has to be the way she puts up with my weirdness
Why would any woman get mixed up with a guy who
Cracks more jokes than a Denny's cook cracks eggs
And can spend countless hours on the computer playing
A game that occasionally makes me scream out obscenities
So on this 4th Valentine spent together, I would like to express
How wonderful, how sweet, how caring you are
Even when you give me the fat lip
For making fun of the way your underwear has holes in it
You fill my days with excitement, laughter and joy
And nights with ate night episodes of Law and Order
And the seldom held snore
'Love from now until my watch breaks

Mi Madre

Millions of memories flood through my mind
Recalling fondly and embracing a woman
Who has helped create for better or worse
What you see before you now
Remembering the trips to the mall
Where my mom would help
Pick outfits that would make me look cool
And warning me of others that
Could make me look dorkier
Smiling as I remember a joke she would make
That I would think of stealing later on
Knowing that in her eyes I could do no wrong
Even when on occasion I let her down
My mind travels to the soccer games
She would watch me play in
And would constantly here her shouts of
Agara la pellota Elmo!
Can't forget all the concerts we went to
Seeing Manilow belt out his sappy ballads
Hearing my moms Spanish voice sing along
A tear runs through my eye
As I remember the call I got from her
Congratulating me on getting my masters
Something she did a long time before I was born
Giggling as I remember our road trips

Where she would plan and guide us
Across the county and never too mad
When dad would blow a turn somewhere
Laughing and making a joke instead
Her beauty starting inside
And radiating all around her
Reminds me of the smile
That would shine and hug me
When she would pick me up from school
Also she is never at a loss for sharing how she felt
Shaking her head when I grew a beard
But still kissing my face regardless
Now as she puts up the biggest battle of her life
She inspires me to live life to the fullest
And never give up the fight
Her grace, love, and spirit
Will stay with me until eternity
You have not lost that beauty
It has truly intensified
You have blessed me more than I can comprehend
I kiss your forehead twice before I go
Knowing there is much more to learn
From a woman who's been
The greatest teacher in my life

Pops

He quietly puts together a jigsaw puzzle
Determining where each piece goes
Methodically finding every match
Slowly Creating a picture
I remember the Star Wars puzzle
We labored on when I was smaller than R2 D2
Many light years ago
Then it happens, floodgates open
Puzzle pieces like storm clouds
Start raining all over me
Here was the guy who taught me about Pong
Who took us on sojourns to the library
The musty smell of library books
I can still clearly smell in my nostrils
And him reading them to me and my brother
Excite us, for another bedtime adventure
Suddenly we are headed to a baseball game
Anaheim stadium full of excitement
Crack of a baseball bat fills the air
Summer voyages across the country
Driving thousands of miles with Mom
As The voluntary GPS, dodging rocks
On a rain slicked highway in the Rockys
There he is coaching my soccer team
Inspiring our team to another victory
From creating a costume for Halloween
To helping me write a paper for a college class
Pops you have always been there for me
And as the years start to pile up
Sadly the words You speak become less
I know you're the reason I became
A pretty good teacher
A not so bad father
And occasionally funny as well
Here you are fighting on
Losing many you love along the way
But inspiring many like you have me
Forever strong,forever my Pops

It's Not Goodbye(Jan's Poem)

Heart full of sorrow more than I can bare
Realizing it more each day you aren't there
However a memory floats inside of my soul
Followed by many more swarming out of control
Your life was a whirlpool of battles and success
Fighting and overcoming always doing your best
You brought your A game to every activity
Reinventing yourself with endless productivity
The world will not be the same without you here
This point is more than crystal clear
You inspired me to do my best
To battle on through every test
You took the grim reaper into overtime
But it was your time to go, no reason or rhyme
So no more sadness no more tears
It always feels that you are near
Everyday I will hear you passing by
But I will never say goodbye

A LITTLE ABOUT THE AUTHOR

Elmo Kelley was born in Fontana California at Kaiser Permanante hospital back in 1971. He is the older of two brothers . Elmo went to public school at St. Francis De sales Catholic church. Elmo attended the University of Riverside California, where he got a Bachelors degree in Human Development. After teaching two years in Riverside, Elmo got a job teaching in Fontana at Cypress Elementary School, where he has taught both second grade and fourth grade for the past twenty-three years.

Elmo has been married to his wife Barbara for twenty -two years and are the parents to two beautiful adopted Children, Kendall, 10 and Carson 6.

Recently Elmo got his Masters degree from Grand Canyon University in curriculum and instruction.

Elmo has been writing poetry for close to thirty years. This is his first book of poetry he has published and is hopefully there will be more volumes to come.

Printed in the United States
by Baker & Taylor Publisher Services